SMART STRATEGIES FOR
BUYING A
CAR

SMART STRATEGIES FOR BUYING A CAR

DANIEL E. HARMON

ROSEN
PUBLISHING®

New York

Published in 2015 by The Rosen Publishing Group, Inc.
29 East 21st Street, New York, NY 10010

First Edition

Library of Congress Cataloging-in-Publication Data

Harmon, Daniel E.
Smart strategies for buying a car/Daniel E. Harmon.
    pages cm.—(Financial security and life success for teens)
Includes bibliographical references and index.
Audience: Grades 7-12.
ISBN 978-1-4777-7622-3 (library bound)—ISBN 978-1-4777-7624-7
(pbk.)—ISBN 978-1-4777-7625-4 (6-pack)
1. Automobiles—Purchasing—United States—Juvenile literature. I. Title.
TL162.H328 2015
629.222029'73—dc23

                                                                2013048266

Manufactured in the United States of America

CONTENTS

INTRODUCTION

Most young drivers have one goal in mind when they think of getting their own vehicle: freedom. They won't have to bum rides and wait on other drivers' schedules. They won't have to bicker with other passengers over where to go first or which radio station to select. If they are bored at a concert or game, they can leave whenever they want. If they hate traveling on interstate highways and congested urban thoroughfares, they can take the back roads and side streets.

Car ownership is one of life's joys as well as one of its major financial investments. For most individuals and families, only a home and a college education cost more. A report at the Energy Trap website points out: "Even when the price of gas is low, the cost of owning a car, insuring it, maintaining it, and buying fuel makes up a big chunk of family budgets." The American Automobile Association (AAA) calculates that the average American who drives a car to work daily should budget approximately $56 in total car expenses for every 100 miles (161 kilometers) driven.

Choosing the best car to suit your needs is an exciting adventure that you will repeat during your life, perhaps many times. Until the major recession that began in 2007, American car owners were trading vehicles approximately every three years. The money crunch sparked a dramatic trend. According to an AutoMD.com survey in 2012, 78

A car salesman goes over terms with a young buyer. The purchase of an automobile is a major transaction that calls for careful questioning and attention to details.

percent of respondents said they plan to keep their vehicle at least ten years "or until it dies." The majority said they intend to get the most from their aging cars, even if the economy improves.

Regardless of how often you trade up, each experience will require careful planning, research, and budgeting. Getting your first car is an especially important educational exercise. It is an opportunity to learn about money management as well as car facts, the many choices available, and the importance of safety. Susie Irvine, spokeswoman for Americans Well-informed on Automobile Retailing Economics (AWARE), explains, "The vehicle shopping and financing process puts key financial concepts into practice for young adults. Teens can calculate how much insurance, gas and routine maintenance will cost and budget for these expenses."

AWARE cites the following valuable skills that teenagers can learn:

- Comparing offers to find the best financing option
- Negotiating terms
- Weighing the choice between purchasing and leasing
- Reading and understanding the fine print in auto sales and warranty contracts
- Questioning the value of extended service contracts and other extras
- Understanding the importance of making payments on time to establish a good credit record

An AAA advisory urges parents and teens to car shop together: "Because liberation and personal mobility may be of primary interest to a young person, it's imperative that parents help address practical considerations in choosing a first vehicle. What most new drivers need is safe, reliable, and affordable transportation. Parents and teens should remember vehicle ownership is a process, not a one-time event."

When you find your ideal car, do not be hasty to sign the papers. Take time—a few hours, if not a day or two—to reconsider your research and weigh all the factors. Be sure it really is the car you want and need.

CHAPTER 1

GETTING AROUND IN MODERN AMERICA

I n centuries past, daily transportation meant walking, riding a horse, or driving a horse-drawn buggy. Some rode bicycles, perhaps as much for recreation and exercise as for practical needs. Trains and streetcars introduced the concept of mass transit.

Henry Ford's manufacturing breakthrough of mass-produced, affordable automobiles revolutionized transportation. By the 1920s, gas-fueled automobiles were becoming the dominant mode of getting around.

CONSIDER ALL YOUR TRANSPORTATION OPTIONS

Before you decide to buy a car, remember that some old-fashioned modes of transportation are still useful. Many people rely on them entirely; some people never bother learn-

An electric car's battery is charged in downtown Portland, Oregon. Auto charging stations are becoming common as the number of electric vehicles increases.

ing to drive. In fact, modern-day energy conservationists look to history as well as to the future for alternatives to gasoline power. Amid growing concerns about pollution and fossil fuel supplies, they urge car buyers to consider every transportation option. Consumers should ask themselves questions such as:

- Where do I go in my daily routine? Is there another option for getting there?
- Do I need to travel alone, or can I carpool with relatives, neighbors, or schoolmates?
- If I had my own car, would it help solve transportation conflicts for my family and me?
- Would the price of car ownership be worth the benefits?

Answers to those questions will determine whether you need to buy a car now or in the future. If you require a car, alternatives to driving should never be overlooked. Walking or bicycling to nearby destinations is enjoyable and healthful. For most city dwellers, mass-transit stops are not far away, and rail and bus systems can get you almost anywhere with few connections. For commutes to school or work, you may join a carpool.

"BUT I REALLY DO NEED A CAR"

In many personal and family situations, those modes of transportation are unavailable, impractical, or come up short for meeting every mobility need. A car is required. Once you've reached that conclusion, the basic steps for pursuing your goal are simple:

- Sit down with a parent or guardian to discuss your need and desire for a car. Ask frankly whether the family financial situation will make a car purchase possible in the foreseeable future. In some families, parents can make a down payment, but the young driver will need to find a way to pay most ongoing expenses.
- Begin lining up your finances. Car ownership, as you will see, entails endless costs—even after the car is paid for.

Teens eager to buy their first vehicle can raise money by working at movie theaters, restaurants, and other retail outlets. Careful budgeting is essential.

Create a budget if you don't have one already. If you have a
job, set aside a substantial portion of your earnings for car
expenses. If you are a student who doesn't work, evaluate
whether you can find time to work part-time.

- Talk to friends and relatives who drive. Find out what they
  like or dislike about their cars.
- Research the auto market. Start a car notebook. Look
  online for charts and reviews comparing car models. Visit
  dealerships to browse and ask questions. Even if you are
  not ready to buy, most sales professionals will talk with
  you. They might even share confidential insights as to why
  certain models have issues that make them less appealing
  to consumers.
- When the time is right, go shopping—accompanied by an
  adult experienced in car shopping.

PLEDGE TO DRIVE RESPONSIBLY

Responsible car ownership goes hand in hand with responsible driving. Before handing them the car keys, parents impress upon young drivers the importance of safety. They worry when their children begin to drive, and with good reason. Among older teens (ages fifteen to twenty), automobile accidents are the leading cause of death, according to the AAA.

The AAA suggests a formal "Parent-Teen Driving Agreement" to be signed by both parties. Posted among the organization's website resources (http://teendriving.aaa.com/files/file/Parent.Teen.Driving.Agreement.pdf), it includes a safety

ARE TEENS TODAY LESS INTERESTED IN CARS?

FROM GENERATION TO GENERATION, TEENAGERS HAVE LONGED TO TAKE THE DRIVER'S SEAT OF THEIR OWN CARS. INTERESTINGLY, YOUNG PEOPLE TODAY SEEM TO BE LESS EXCITED ABOUT CAR OWNERSHIP. STUDIES BY AUTOTRADER.COM IN 2013 INDICATED THAT MILLENNIALS (BORN BETWEEN THE EARLY 1980S AND EARLY 2000S) GENERALLY ARE NOT AS EAGER TO GET DRIVER'S LICENSES AND CARS AS TEENS WERE IN TIMES PAST.

RESEARCH SUGGESTS THAT A REASON FOR THIS DIMINISHED INTEREST IS THE POPULARITY OF SOCIAL MEDIA. THE INTERNET MAKES IT POSSIBLE FOR YOUNG PEOPLE TO INTERACT SOCIALLY VIA SMARTPHONES, TABLETS, AND NOTEBOOK COMPUTERS. THEY CAN HANG OUT CONSTANTLY WITH MANY FRIENDS AT ONCE, WHEREVER THEY ARE, BY TEXT MESSAGE, E-MAIL, AND FACE-TO-FACE VIDEO CHAT.

THEIR PARENTS AND GRANDPARENTS DID NOT ENJOY THOSE AVENUES OF INSTANT, ANYWHERE/EVERYWHERE COMMUNICATION. WHEN THEY WERE YOUNG, THEY HUNG OUT AT SCHOOL PARKING LOTS, DRIVE-IN RESTAURANTS, AND OTHER GATHERING PLACES. CARS GOT THEM THERE AND GOT THEM HOME. A CAR WAS THE TICKET TO SOCIAL FREEDOM. BECAUSE SO MUCH OF TODAY'S SOCIAL INTERACTION IS DONE REMOTELY, CARS MAY HAVE BECOME LESS NECESSARY.

checklist with recurring checkpoints for monitoring the progress of the beginning driver. Violations of driving rules result in the loss of privileges for a specified time. For example, getting a speeding ticket or failing to make passengers wear seatbelts can be penalized by weeks or months of lost privileges. Driving under the influence, even if no arrest occurs, might take away the car for a year or longer.

Parental guidance and assistance are important in introducing teens to driving responsibilities and car ownership. Here, a mother familiarizes her daughter with dashboard controls and indicators.

The AAA says guidelines "help communicate to teens that their family takes the learning-to-drive process seriously." The organization urges weekly meetings to review supervised and unsupervised driving activities and to decide on upcoming driving lessons and plans.

PARK IT WHEN YOU DON'T NEED IT

Environmentalists encourage Americans to drive as little as possible. Dwindling natural fuel sources are one concern. Poisonous emissions are another. Heavy highway traffic pollutes the atmosphere and impairs the health of humans and wildlife.

Realistically, most families in the United States need at least one car. Many families need a vehicle for each driver. Still, they should drive conservatively. Errands—visits to the supermarket, library, and a friend's home—can be combined into one gas-saving excursion. Why drive to your grandparents' home if it's only two blocks away?

Young drivers should develop responsible driving habits at the outset. Responsibilities include driving safely and being mindful of other drivers, maintaining a safe and efficient vehicle, and driving only when necessary.

MYTHS AND FACTS

MYTH: DRIVERS ARE SAFER WITH FRIENDS RIDING WITH THEM. IT TAKES AWAY THE TEMPTATION TO TEXT WHILE DRIVING AND HELPS ALERT THE DRIVER TO POTENTIAL HAZARDS.

FACT: THAT IS NOT THE CASE WITH TEENAGE DRIVERS. AN AAA STUDY PUBLISHED IN 2012 FOUND THAT THE PRESENCE OF YOUNG PASSENGERS (AND NO ADULT PASSENGERS) INCREASES THE RISK OF TEEN DRIVER FATALITIES. THE RISK OF A SIXTEEN- OR SEVENTEEN-YEAR-OLD DRIVER DYING IN A CRASH REPORTEDLY INCREASES BY 44 PERCENT WHEN THERE IS ONE YOUNGER-THAN-TWENTY-ONE PASSENGER. THE RISK OF THE DRIVER'S DEATH INCREASES WITH THE NUMBER OF YOUNG PASSENGERS IN THE CAR. "IN CONTRAST," THE STUDY FOUND, "CARRYING ADULT PASSENGERS SIGNIFICANTLY REDUCES THE RISK OF CRASH INVOLVEMENT."

MYTH: YOUNG DRIVERS ARE SAFER THAN OLDER DRIVERS BECAUSE THEY ARE MORE ALERT AND AGILE AT THE WHEEL.

FACT: ALTHOUGH MENTAL REACTIONS AND PHYSICAL MOVEMENTS BEGIN TO SLOW AT A CERTAIN STAGE IN LIFE, TEEN DRIVERS ARE MORE ACCIDENT-PRONE. THE INSURANCE INSTITUTE FOR HIGHWAY SAFETY REPORTS THAT TEENAGE DRIVERS ARE TWO TO THREE TIMES MORE LIKELY THAN ADULTS TO BE INVOLVED IN AUTO CRASHES.

MYTH: LABOR DAY WEEKEND IS THE TIME TO GET THE BEST PRICE ON A NEW CAR. THAT IS JUST BEFORE THE NEW MODELS COME OUT, WHEN DEALERS ARE CLEARING THEIR LOTS OF LAST YEAR'S UNSOLD BUT STILL "NEW" CARS.

FACT: THE "BEST TIME TO BUY A NEW CAR" ALSO HAS BEEN ATTRIB-
UTED TO THE LAST WEEK IN OCTOBER, "BLACK FRIDAY" (THE DAY AFTER
THANKSGIVING), AND THE END OF THE CALENDAR YEAR. AUTOMAKERS
INTRODUCE NEW CARS AT DIFFERENT TIMES. TRADITIONALLY, LATE
SUMMER AND AUTUMN HAVE BEEN THE RELEASE SEASON. BUT MANU-
FACTURERS DO NOT MAKE INTRODUCTIONS ON THE SAME DATES EVERY
YEAR, NOR DO THEY RELEASE ALL THE NEW MODELS IN THEIR LINES
SIMULTANEOUSLY.

IT IS TRUE THAT DEALERS ADVERTISE CLOSEOUT DISCOUNTS
ON MODELS THAT ARE ABOUT TO BECOME OUTDATED. BUYERS SHOULD
BE CAREFUL, HOWEVER. SOME OF THOSE CARS HAVE LINGERED ON THE
LOT BECAUSE THEY HAVE DUBIOUS REPUTATIONS IN TERMS OF VALUE
AND PERFORMANCE.

NOTE, TOO, THAT CAR SELLING IS HIGHLY COMPETITIVE. LOCAL
AND REGIONAL DEALERS FREQUENTLY LAUNCH APPEALING SALES CAM-
PAIGNS, OFTEN COINCIDING WITH HOLIDAY WEEKENDS THROUGHOUT
THE YEAR.

CHAPTER 2

ENTERING THE AUTO MARKETPLACE

A merican consumers are barraged by car advertisements. They are tempted to buy or trade when they don't need to. A car purchase shouldn't be rushed into. A bad decision can bring long-term headaches.

THE STATE OF THE AUTO MARKET

Until recent years, many American consumers were willing to obtain a loan every three or four years to trade cars. They were making car payments most of their adult lives. Millions of buyers chose cars as status symbols. They paid extra for vehicles of a certain make, style, or color, or with excessive engine power and unnecessary frills.

That changed with the worldwide economic downturn beginning in 2007. Consumers were forced to spend more carefully. They began driving their cars longer before trading. Today, it is not unusual to see advertisements for used cars with more than 200,000 miles (321,869 km) on the odometer, still in drivable condition.

Industry observers say car owners also have become more conscientious about caring for their automobiles. At the same time, the quality of automobiles has improved. Cars are built better today than those a quarter century ago. There are two main reasons.

- The global economy has intensified competition among automakers. They pay close attention to customer satisfaction surveys and ratings. To keep their products running longer with fewer breakdowns, they use higher-grade critical parts.

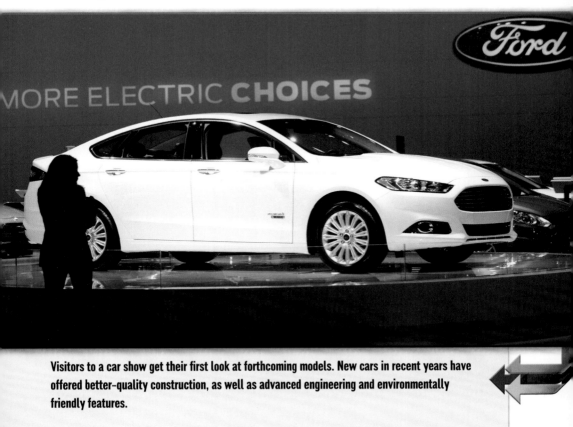

Visitors to a car show get their first look at forthcoming models. New cars in recent years have offered better-quality construction, as well as advanced engineering and environmentally friendly features.

- The Environmental Protection Agency (EPA) has strengthened regulations on auto emissions. This has led manufacturers to design engine systems that process less oil, which reduces overall wear. Other design factors have improved, such as rust and corrosion protection.

Another reason people are keeping their cars longer is an upward trend in new car prices. By 2012, TrueCar.com found that prices for new cars were averaging $30,500. Typical families in most of North America's largest cities could not afford to obtain the average-priced new car without imposing a risky strain on their budgets, according to a 2013 auto affordability survey by Interest.com.

New car prices are going up largely because state-of-the-art frills are in demand. Air-conditioning and power steering and windows—once considered extravagances—are expected. Competing automakers advertise electronic infotainment units, rearview cameras, and other gadgets designed for convenience and safety. One result of rising prices has been a trend among consumers to buy smaller, more economical cars.

CHOOSING STANDARD FEATURES AND EXTRAS

The distinction between standard features and options in today's automobiles is hazy. Heating, air-conditioning, and a radio—all of them extras in generations past—are basic. Beyond those, most non-necessities technically are considered

SURVEY: TEENAGERS TODAY ARE SAVVY CAR SHOPPERS

RESEARCH SUGGESTS THAT MOST TEENAGERS GO FOR STYLISH LUXURY CARS WITH ADVANCED EQUIPMENT. BUT MOST RECOGNIZE THAT FOR NOW, THOSE CARS ARE BEYOND THEIR MEANS.

A 2013 STUDY BY AUTOTRADER.COM TITLED "THE NEXT GENERATION CAR BUYER" INDICATES THAT YOUNG BUYERS ARE BRAND-CONSCIOUS. AUDI, BMW, AND MERCEDES TYPIFY THE CAR MAKES THEY FIND MOST ATTRACTIVE. MOST TEENS SURVEYED, THOUGH, SAID THEY PROBABLY WILL OPT FOR A MAINSTREAM CAR—NOT JUST BECAUSE IT'S LESS EXPENSIVE, BUT BECAUSE THEY REALIZE IT'S MORE PRACTICAL.

ADDITIONAL FINDINGS OF THE STUDY CREDIT TEENS WITH PERHAPS BETTER CAR-BUYING SENSE THAN PRECEDING GENERATIONS. THEY RESEARCH THE CAR MARKET AND LISTEN TO THE EXPERIENCES AND RECOMMENDATIONS OF OTHERS. THE AUTOTRADER.COM REPORT STATES, "THEY'RE ALSO MOST LIKELY TO BE FIRST INTRODUCED TO THEIR CAR OF CHOICE THROUGH A FAMILY MEMBER OR FRIEND, AS OPPOSED TO BABY BOOMERS WHO ARE MOST LIKELY TO BE FIRST INTRODUCED TO THEIR CAR ON THE DEALERSHIP LOT." ALTHOUGH THEY ENJOY EXPLORING CAR LOTS AND ASKING QUESTIONS OF SALES STAFF, THEY'RE TURNED OFF BY HIGH-PRESSURE SELLING TACTICS, ACCORDING TO THE STUDY.

options. But many car shoppers today expect power steering, cruise control, and antilock brakes. Luxuries today such
as keyless door unlocking, adjustable steering columns, side
airbags, built-in GPS navigation, and rear-seat entertainment
devices come installed on many new cars.

An interesting decision is whether to drive with an automatic or manual (stick shift) transmission. Automatics, as the

Many new automobiles today come with Global Positioning System (GPS) technology built into
the dashboards. Satellite-guided GPS devices steer drivers to unfamiliar destinations.

term implies, are simpler. You merely put the gearstick in "drive" or "reverse" to go forward (at any speed) or backward. Lower forward gears are available to help the engine power the car up sharp inclines or pull heavy loads. A manual transmission, by contrast, has between three and six forward gears and requires a foot-operated clutch to shift between gears. When navigating through slow/fast traffic situations, the driver constantly changes to the gear best suited for the moment.

Manual transmissions were dominant until the mid-1900s. Today, most new cars come with automatic transmissions. Manual systems are hard to find in new cars, except in sports cars and subcompacts. Most young drivers learn to drive with automatic transmissions. Many never learn to operate manual gears, preferring the convenience of automatic transmissions.

However, manual transmissions are more economical to operate. *Consumer Reports* in 2013 found that "a stick shift can improve gas mileage by a notable 2 to 5 mpg [miles per gallon], compared with an automatic transmission, and can cut a car's price by $800 to $1,200. Manual transmissions also improve acceleration, sometimes significantly."

Their declining popularity is an economic drawback. The magazine points out, "Because relatively few buyers are choosing manual transmissions, the car could be harder to sell later."

BUYING A CAR IS INVESTING IN A RELIC

In twenty-first-century society, new becomes old all too quickly. The smartphone you buy next week will be an antique next year.

"WHAT IF I END UP WITH A LEMON?"

A FEAR OF ALL CAR BUYERS IS THAT THE VEHICLE THEY SELECT WILL TURN OUT TO BE A LEMON. LEMONS—CARS WITH FREQUENT OR RECURRING PROBLEMS—SOMETIMES ARE HARD TO RECOGNIZE WHILE CAR SHOPPING, EVEN IN TEST DRIVES. THE SEQUENCE OF WOES MAY NOT BEGIN UNTIL YOU'VE DRIVEN THE VEHICLE SEVERAL THOUSAND MILES.

BUYERS HAVE LEGAL REMEDIES IN STATE "LEMON LAWS." MANUFACTURERS OR DEALERS MUST BUY BACK OR REPLACE VEHICLES THAT ARE PROVED TO REPEATEDLY FAIL.

USED AND LEASED CARS ARE NOT COVERED IN SOME STATES. TO FIND OUT THE DETAILS IN YOUR STATE, GOOGLE "LEMON LAW" FOR A LIST OF EXPLANATORY RESOURCES. ONE POPULAR SOURCE OF INFORMATION FOR CONSUMERS IS THE U.S. BETTER BUSINESS BUREAU (BBB). TO FIND THE BBB'S LEMON LAW FOR YOUR STATE, TYPE THE WEB LINK: WWW.BBB.ORG/US/STATE-NAME-LEMON-LAW. FOR EXAMPLE, THE ADDRESS FOR OHIO INFORMATION IS WWW.BBB.ORG/US/OHIO-LEMON-LAW; FOR NEW MEXICO, IT'S WWW.BBB.ORG/US/NEW-MEXICO-LEMON-LAW.

Cars last much longer, but they are impermanent. The minute you buy a car, it begins to lose value—even before you drive it.

How can that be? It is because at the point of sale, the car technically becomes a used car. As the mileage/kilometrage and age increase in coming months and years, the car will depreciate in resale value.

The *Kelley Blue Book* is the standard reference on car values. The online app shows different views of various automobiles and provides reviews, safety ratings, and comparisons.

Kelley Blue Book
THE TRUSTED RESOURCE

News & Reviews

My Next Car

My Current Car

Nearby Dealers

Recently Viewed Cars

view all

2013 Chevrolet
Volt Sedan

2012 Mercedes-
Benz E-Class

2013 Audi A8
3.0T Sedan

     4

The *Kelley Blue Book* is the standard guide used by auto buyers and sellers to determine the approximate value of every car by make, model, and year. An online calculator (www. kbb.com) quickly gives you the fair market value of all new cars in your ZIP code area. A companion calculator shows used car values. For used car research, enter the year, make, model, style, and basic options. Also enter the purchasing type: private party, if buying from an individual; suggested retail, if buying from a dealer; or certified preowned (CPO), if the car has CPO status. The calculator then displays the comparative prices for that particular vehicle, depending on whether it is in excellent, very good, good, or fair condition. The *Kelley Blue Book*'s online calculator is a useful tool to find out what price to expect when you are ready to sell or trade. The *Kelley Blue Book* will become a standard reference in your car shopping.

10 GREAT QUESTIONS
TO ASK A USED CAR SELLER

1. Has the car been wrecked or severely damaged by weather?
2. Why is your asking price significantly higher than the *Kelley Blue Book* value?
3. Why is your asking price significantly lower than the *Kelley Blue Book* value? Is something wrong with the car?
4. Does the car require any special servicing or any pricey replacement parts?
5. Is this car model noted for any particular kind of breakdown?
6. May I take the car across town to our family's longtime maintenance shop for an inspection? If not, may I bring our mechanic here to inspect the car?
7. May I contact the previous owner?
8. Are the service and repair records for the car available for me to look at?
9. What's the expected mileage/kilometrage for a set of tires on this model and style of car, assuming normal driving conditions and proper tire maintenance?
10. What is the return policy, in case I encounter a pre-existing problem with the car?

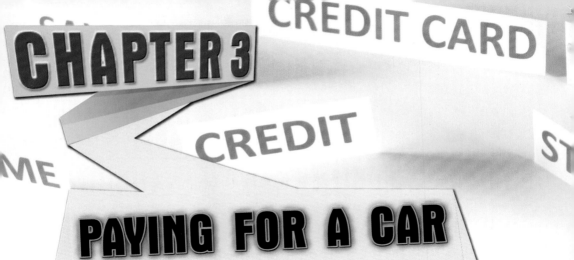

CHAPTER 3

PAYING FOR A CAR

nder ideal circumstances, a car buyer works and saves money until he or she has enough to pay the full price of the car at the time of purchase. Most people, though, are compelled to buy cars when they do not have sufficient cash on hand. They must obtain car loans from banks or mortgage companies.

Teenagers typically need help from parents to buy their first car. A parent may agree to make the down payment, for example, if the teen agrees to earn enough money to make monthly payments or pay for gas, maintenance, and other ongoing costs. Whatever the arrangement, the teen should use the experience to learn about the costs and responsibilities of car ownership.

WHAT THE DIFFERENT WINDOW STICKERS MEAN

When you examine the window sticker on a car at a dealership, you probably will see two or more itemized lists and prices. The bottom-line prices might vary by more than a thousand dollars. Which is your actual cost?

- The invoice price of a new automobile is the amount the manufacturer charges the car dealer. This price obviously is lower than what the car buyer will pay.

New cars in showrooms usually display more than one sheet of specifications and prices. The shopper can compare the manufacturer's invoice price with the dealer's asking price.

- The Monroney sticker by law is displayed on all new cars. It specifies engine and transmission details, itemizes the car's standard equipment and optional features (with the costs of each option), and estimates the expected fuel mileage/kilometrage. It publishes the manufacturer's suggested retail price (MSRP). The Monroney sticker also contains warranty details.
- The sticker price is the actual sales price. In almost all cases, the dealer's sales professional is willing to negotiate downward.

To make money, dealers must charge customers more than the invoice price. How much above the invoice price they can negotiate with customers will determine their profit.

A common sales tactic is to advertise vehicles for only a few dollars "above invoice." As the end of a sales season approaches, dealers may even offer existing cars for "below invoice" to clear the lot and make way for new models. Rarely do dealers actually lose money in these transactions. Typically, they receive compensation from the manufacturer, known as a rebate.

COST FACTORS INVOLVED IN BORROWING

New car financing frequently is arranged at the dealership. The sales and finance employees try to help the buyer find a lending company and loan plan within the buyer's budget. If they succeed, the lending institution literally buys the car from the dealer and acquires the title. The car purchaser then buys the car title from the lending company over time. During the payback period, the purchaser possesses and drives the car but does not legally own it. If at some point the buyer falters in monthly payments, the lender holding the title can take over (repossess) the vehicle.

Auto loans are often arranged through the dealership. Buyers can also obtain personal loans and use credit cards. They must be cautious and avoid high-interest indebtedness.

The following are loan factors to consider:

- Down payment. In most cases, the buyer should expect to pay a certain amount at the time of purchase. The amount required depends on factors such as what the seller is willing to accept (based largely on how badly the seller needs to make the sale) and the buyer's credit rating. This down payment may be several thousand dollars or as little as several hundred dollars. If the buyer is trading in an old car, the approximate value of the traded vehicle may be accepted as the down payment.
- Loan amount. The down payment and any rebate are subtracted from the negotiated selling price. The remainder is the amount that must be borrowed.
- Loan period. This is the length of time allowed to pay the loan—typically five years (sixty months). Loan periods in many situations are decided by the buyer's budget.
- Interest rate. The lending firm must earn a profit on the money it lends. It does this by charging interest on the loan. Interest rates trend up and down over the years; the country's overall economy ultimately affects lending. Some buyers pay 10 percent or higher in interest; others pay little or nothing. Generally, purchasers with the highest credit scores can obtain the best interest rates. Interest rates also are affected by the market; lower interest rates are offered at times to stimulate sluggish sales.

The greater the down payment and the less the loan, the less the buyer ultimately will pay in interest. The length of the loan and the interest rate also determine the total interest costs. Loans that are paid back quickly will incur less total interest. If you have a five-year loan and can pay it off a year or six months early, you can save substantial interest.

Amortization programs (available free as computer software and smartphone apps) can tabulate all the cost factors. They can show the buyer in advance precisely how much monthly payments will be, depending on the amount borrowed, payback period, and interest rate. The buyer can examine different scenarios and decide which best satisfies the present and future personal budget—and whether the purchase is possible at all.

ASK YOUR FRIENDS FOR HELP

Need help raising the cash for your first car purchase? You might be able to get some of your social networking friends to chip in. Online auto buying services and some auto manufacturers offer programs in which a prospective car buyer can solicit friends to contribute online.

One example is Dodge Dart Registry (www.dodgedartregistry. com). It facilitates participation in a young buyer's purchase ambition by involving online friends to help pay for the car. In essence, Dodge explains: "Pick out the features you want in your new Dart and then invite friends and family to sponsor individual parts of the car. You can raise a portion of the cost of a new Dart or the full price. Then all you have to do is go to a dealership and pick it up."

Some online services let young people open a form of car-purchase savings account, into which friends can contribute. Increasingly, graduates and newlyweds are requesting deposits into their car accounts as gifts.

BUDGETING EXPLAINS EVERYTHING

A car purchase may be something you should put off until you go to college, or later. On the other hand, it may be a useful investment now, if you can obtain a loan. In either case, you need to establish a budget for all your expenses, outlining the car portion of your budget in detail. Your budget will tell you whether a car purchase is doable and, if so, how it will impact your life financially.

Budgets seem baffling to many young people—and many adults. It boils down to the simplest of monetary factors: how much you earn versus how much you spend. If you detail your earnings and expenses, you can see exactly what's happening with your money.

The key, of course, is income. Many teens have lucrative part-time jobs; a few manage full-time jobs while still in school. Some can afford to make the down payment on a car and pay all the ensuing expenses. In every circumstance, a sound budget is crucial for keeping the plan on track.

A high school or college student should take into account all the costs of owning and operating a car (discussed later). Bear in mind that car expenses represent just one section of the budget. The budget might reveal that a car purchase will devour most of the income, leaving the student with little extra money to "have a life." In that instance, the budgeter may decide to postpone buying a car until completing college and going to work full-time.

A careful study of personal budget figures can determine whether a car purchase is feasible and how the various auto costs would affect other budget categories.

On the other hand, hard work and careful spending habits can make car ownership possible while still in high school. Some teens find that if they apply themselves to work steady hours part-time and discipline themselves to save most of their earnings, they can earn enough for a car down payment within a year, or a matter of months.

Remember that the car expense details comprise just one budget category. All other routine expenses, as well as emergencies, must be taken into account. Other financial demands might combine to make it very difficult to buy a car.

The cost of car ownership can be budgeted with reasonable accuracy. You can calculate how much you are paying for gas each month, on average. You know how frequently you must have the oil changed and approximately what it will cost. You can budget for a new set of tires every three or four years.

Unexpected expenditures are inevitable. A headlight goes out and must be replaced. A problem with the emission system requires a new catalytic converter or exhaust. A faulty thermostat causes overheating. The battery dies. The side-view mirror shatters when you slam the door too hard. A severe tear mars the upholstery. The radio/CD unit goes on the blink. The car fails to start and you must buy a new alternator. Faulty repairs are a common complaint among car owners.

PROS AND CONS OF LEASING

Auto leasing appeals to many prospective buyers, including some young people. The apparent benefits are seemingly low monthly payments and the fact that you are riding in a nice new car. But lease agreements are designed for a particular segment of the auto market, and that segment does not really include young buyers.

Many companies that provide business cars for employees prefer to lease, rather than buy them outright. Some organizations give employees a specified monthly car allowance for business-related travel. An employee may choose to apply the

CREATE A CAR COST WORKSHEET

YOU CAN KEEP RECORDS OF YOUR CAR OWNERSHIP EXPENSES IN VARIOUS WAYS. SOME CAREFUL BUDGETERS KEEP PRINTED RECEIPTS OF EVERY PURCHASE THEY MAKE IN A MONTHLY OR QUARTERLY ENVELOPE. AT THE END OF THE PERIOD, THEY SEPARATE THE RECEIPTS INTO CATEGORIES (CAR, HOUSING, UTILITIES, FOOD, CLOTHES, MEDICAL EXPENSES, EMERGENCIES, ENTERTAINMENT, ETC.). THEY TOTAL THE EXPENDITURES IN EACH CATEGORY AND ENTER THE NUMBERS IN THEIR ONGOING BUDGET.

IT IS AN EXCELLENT HABIT TO ACCOUNT FOR EVERYTHING YOU BUY. IT ALSO IS A GOOD IDEA TO SAVE AUTO-RELATED RECEIPTS THROUGHOUT THE OWNERSHIP PERIOD. AT THE SAME TIME, A COMPUTERIZED RECORD-KEEPING SYSTEM CAN BE VERY USEFUL IN KEEPING YOU APPRISED OF CAR COSTS. AN ORGANIZED WORKSHEET WILL SHOW YOU QUICKLY, AT ANY TIME, WHETHER YOUR AUTOMOTIVE EXPENSES ARE STAYING IN LINE WITH YOUR GENERAL BUDGET OR ARE GETTING YOU INTO TROUBLE.

LINE ITEMS IN THE WORKSHEET SHOULD INCLUDE LOAN PAYMENTS, GAS, MAINTENANCE, REPLACEMENT PARTS, INSURANCE, TAXES, FEES, AND ADD-ONS (NEW AUDIO SYSTEM SPEAKERS, WINDSHIELD SUN SCREEN, PORTABLE GPS, TRAVEL MAPS, AIR FRESHENERS, AND SO FORTH). YOU CAN ALSO ESTIMATE MONTHLY OR QUARTERLY DEPRECIATION, BASED ON *KELLEY BLUE BOOK* VALUES.

money toward a vehicle lease or toward the purchase or maintenance of a personal car.

For personal use, most individual consumers are better off buying instead of leasing. After considering all the factors, they find that a purchase makes economic sense. Bear in mind these points:

- To begin with, the leasing firm probably will require the lessor to be at least twenty-one years old.
- You are bound for the term of the lease contract—even if you quickly decide you don't like the car. If you insist on terminating the lease early or exchanging cars, you almost certainly will have to pay a significant fee.
- You may be required to buy additional insurance.
- Under most lease plans, the allowable mileage/kilometrage per month or per year is limited. Exceeding the limit will result in added costs.
- Car buying represents an investment. Once the car is paid for, you own valuable property for as long as you continue to drive it. Your next car dealer will allow you at least some value for it (probably enough for a down payment, if no more) when you eventually shop for another car. But when a lease contract expires, you turn in the car, own nothing, and have to make new driving arrangements with no car to trade.

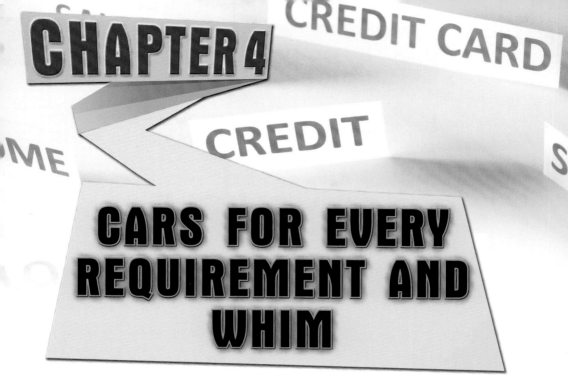

CHAPTER 4

CARS FOR EVERY REQUIREMENT AND WHIM

Most shoppers look for a vehicle that best meets their transportation needs. Naturally, they also want one that suits their personal style. Budgets often permit one objective, but not both.

For economy-minded buyers, auto consultants cite two basic traits to consider: small and unsophisticated. "Small" relates not only to body size but also to the size of the car engine. In most cases, four-cylinder engines get much better mileage/kilometrage than more powerful engines with six or eight cylinders.

"Unsophisticated" does not mean you cannot buy a car that has power windows and a nice sound system (although such items add to the sales price). In the long run, it means selecting a less expensive make and model with a proven record of driving efficiency. Generally, the pricier the make, the more expensive each replacement part will be. Ordinary service costs for luxury and sports cars also tend to be higher.

The AAA lists five main considerations in buying a car for teenagers: vehicle type, safety, affordability, reliability, and familiarity.

TYPE OF VEHICLE

There are many from which to choose: cabriolet, subcompact, compact, sport utility vehicle (SUV), multipurpose vehicle

Buyers find many categories of vehicles from which to choose. Many young drivers find trucks especially appealing, although safety-wise, trucks have a worse tendency to overturn than sedans.

(MPV), station wagon, luxury, sport, etc. An AAA advisory states, "Newer sedans make good choices for teens. Sports cars or other high-performance vehicles may tempt some teens to speed or drive recklessly." The AAA also notes that SUVs and vans are more top-heavy than mid-size sedans and thus are more prone to roll over.

Trucks are popular among young drivers. They are handy for transporting musical and recreational equipment. College students find them very useful for their frequent housing moves, as well as for transporting project materials required for certain courses. A student with a truck can make lots of friends on campus.

Many teens, especially females, consider trucks safer than cars. It may be a false sense of security, though. Studies have shown that pickup trucks, like SUVs, handle more clumsily than sedans and have a worse tendency to roll over. Another drawback is that many truck models are notably less fuel-efficient than small and mid-size autos. Cautious, defensive driving is paramount regardless of the vehicle.

SAFETY

Responsive handling, excellent tires and brakes, and innovative lighting contribute to the vehicle's overall safety. Special features include antilock brakes, both front and side airbags, headrests that can be adjusted and locked, and daytime running lights. Electronic stability control (ESC) enhances driver control of the vehicle; it has been shown to reduce single-car rollover accidents by as much as 70 percent.

AFFORDABILITY

The AAA observes, "A new car may be the most desirable option, but not within your budget. A certified used car might offer similar peace of mind at a lower price."

Certified used vehicles are thoroughly inspected. Many come with impressive warranties. Depending on the young buyer's needs, a certified used car may be the best value.

Fuel efficiency will be vital. Over time, the difference of just one mile or kilometer per gallon, on the average, can add up to more than a thousand dollars in fuel costs. You might save additionally by shopping carefully for car insurance.

Certified used vehicles are worth considering, the AAA states, even though they may cost more than similar models that are uncertified. Typically, certified cars have relatively low mileage and had just one previous owner, or were lease vehicles.

RELIABILITY

Research the maintenance and repair ratings of both new and used cars. Study the warranty. For used cars, try to obtain maintenance and repair records and have the vehicle inspected by a mechanic you or your parents know. Although some used cars with high mileage/kilometrage may still run fine, parts inevitably wear out. Also, older cars probably lack some of the latest safety features.

FAMILIARITY

The AAA points out that it's a good idea for a young driver to get a car of approximately the same type, size, and power as the one he or she learned to drive in. Otherwise, "plan extra practice hours with the new vehicle."

Read the owner's manual. Owners who are thoroughly familiar with their vehicles can perform various adjustments, maintenance, and repairs or part replacements themselves, saving money.

NEW OR USED?

Some consumers never buy used cars. They believe that in most cases, when you buy used, you're "buying someone else's problems." It stands to reason that the best used cars on the road are not for sale; their owners are happy with them. The

Buyers of used cars should try to determine whether a vehicle has been affected by a natural event such as flooding, which may result in permanent damage.

ones that are for sale are being offered for a reason. Repairs become more frequent and more serious as automobiles age. Not all used cars are lemons, though.

Other buyers favor used vehicles. They have found that by shopping carefully and asking hard questions, they can save money and still get an excellent, long-lasting ride.

The car's history is important. A car with 200,000 miles (321,869 km) may be a good buy if it has been driven responsibly and maintained properly. A car with only 50,000 miles (80,467 km) may be a dud if it has been wrecked, damaged, or driven recklessly or if the owner has neglected oil changes and other maintenance. Was the previous owner an aggressive driver prone to vigorous acceleration and braking and to fender benders and collisions? Or a thrill seeker who delighted in spinouts and going airborne over speed bumps?

Natural events can affect the quality and life span of a used car. Prolonged driving in coastal regions can result in saltwater corrosion of the underside and finish. Flooding can have a long-term impact. Rain leakage, common in convertibles, can result in water accumulation that erodes the floor pan.

The seller of a problem vehicle may be less than honest with prospective buyers. Buyers should engage a trusted mechanic to examine the vehicle for signs of abuse or major repairs.

WHEELING AND DEALING

Expect to negotiate. In almost every situation, the seller is willing to come down from the asking price (the sticker

WHAT DOES "CERTIFIED USED" MEAN?

MANY CAR DEALERS NOW ADVERTISE "CERTIFIED" USED VEHICLES. THESE CARS ARE METHODICALLY INSPECTED, TESTED, AND REFURBISHED. ALTHOUGH PREOWNED, SOME OF THEM ARE LIKE NEW AND ARE SOLD WITH ATTRACTIVE, LONG-TERM WARRANTIES. CONSEQUENTLY, THEY COST MORE THAN ORDINARY USED CARS OF THEIR CLASS AND MODEL. MORE AND MORE CONSUMERS, THOUGH, ARE REASSURED BY THE CERTIFICATION AND OPT FOR CERTIFIED USED CARS, RATHER THAN FACTORY-NEW AUTOS.

THE AAA SUGGESTS THAT A LATE-MODEL USED AUTO "MAY PROVIDE THE BEST BALANCE BETWEEN SAFETY AND PRICE."

price). For that reason and others, the young buyer should be accompanied by an adult who is experienced in car buying. A knowledgeable adult can help you make the best deal.

Be wary of special offers. Auto sellers sometimes offer deep discounts on new car models that are not selling well. It is possible to acquire a fine vehicle for a remarkably low price in this way. However, those cars may have disappointing performance and low consumer ratings.

Self-discipline is a critical factor for a young car buyer. No matter how attractive a deal seems, do not exceed your budget, either for a down payment or for monthly loan payments. It may be true that for just a few dollars more per month, you can have a much nicer car. To make that work, though, you will have to sacrifice in other areas of your budget. Are you willing to do that?

WARRANTIES—A MORASS OF FINE PRINT

All new cars and many used cars are sold with warranties. There are numerous types. Kelsey Mays, writing at Cars. com, observes, "In all, a car can leave the dealership with 10 or more warranties—which can be a mess for its new owner to wade through."

Under typical bumper-to-bumper warranties, vehicles are guaranteed to not break down for a specified period of time or number of miles (kilometers) driven. For example, the basic warranty may last for 50,000 miles (80,467 km) or three years. If the car breaks down while under warranty, most or all of the repair expenses will cost the owner nothing. The standard manufacturer's warranty, perhaps with additional coverage offered by the dealer, is usually all you need. However, you should read the warranty before buying. Some warranties do not cover certain parts or certain types of malfunction.

When you sit down to discuss and sign the contract, the dealer might offer supplemental or extended warranties for an extra charge. Some extended warranties could turn out to be very useful, covering major fixes for as long as you're likely to own the car. But pay special attention to the wording of extended warranties. They may exclude certain types of repairs that were covered under the original warranty—repairs that become necessary with aging vehicles.

Before signing a purchase contract, the buyer should go over all the warranty conditions with the sales representative. A dealer's supplemental warranty may be unnecessary.

Common supplemental warranties include special coverage of the powertrain (engine, transmission, drive shaft, and related parts), tires, battery, emission system, and airbags. You can also buy additional roadside assistance features.

Used car sales are more limited in their warranty options. Some used cars, though, are under original or extended warranties that can be transferred to the new owner.

The Federal Trade Commission (FTC) in a consumer advisory points out the difference between an auto warranty and service contract. The warranty is included in the purchase price. A service contract is "an add-on that might not be worth the price. Some service contracts duplicate the warranty coverage that the manufacturer provides; some cover only part of the product; and some make it nearly impossible to get repairs when you need them."

The FTC notes that it may be better to put into a savings account the money you would spend for extended coverage. "If you need repairs, you'll have your savings to fall back on. And if you don't need repairs, you'll have a little extra money in the bank."

Young, first-time buyers in particular are sometimes persuaded to buy unneeded coverage. That is another reason why the assistance of a parent or other car-savvy adult is important when making the purchase.

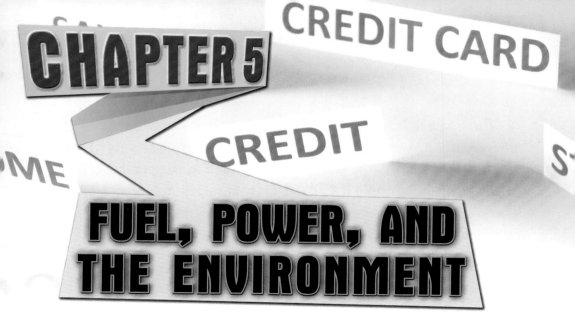

CHAPTER 5

FUEL, POWER, AND THE ENVIRONMENT

Until 1973, almost all Americans assumed they would be driving gasoline-fueled cars all their lives. There had been experiments with electric and other kinds of automotive power. None of the experiments, however, had produced a way to make those vehicles affordable or practical to drive from day to day.

Alternative fuels and power systems became big news in autumn of that year. A military crisis in the Middle East affected the whole world. Oil-producing countries in that region temporarily halted shipments of petroleum to the United States and other Western nations. The impact was felt immediately. Long lines of angry motorists formed at gas stations. Heated confrontations erupted. Gas, in preciously limited supply, was rationed. In some places, drivers were sold only a few gallons at a time. In others, the ending number of the license plate determined which days of the week gas could be bought.

The situation did not last long, but it made Americans think deeply about the way energy is produced and consumed. They began to realize that although Earth stores enough oil and natural gas to last many years, the supplies are not endless. In a few generations, severe problems will occur unless energy consumption patterns change dramatically.

During the same period, environmentalists were making people aware of the harm caused by the use of certain types of energy. Petroleum-based products such as gasoline in particular pose environmental hazards.

PETROLEUM FUELS

Auto gasoline, diesel fuel, jet fuel, engine oil, and certain other fuel and lubricating products are refined from petroleum.

"Regular" pump fuels are the most common. "Plus" fuels are a higher grade and may yield better mileage. Diesel fuels can be used only in cars with diesel engines.

Petroleum is known as a fossil fuel, formed underground by Earth's internal heat and pressure on dead organisms over long periods of time. Coal is also a fossil fuel.

The burning of petroleum and other fossil fuels—most notably in vehicles, factories, and homes—releases carbon dioxide into the atmosphere. Carbon dioxide is a poisonous greenhouse gas that contributes greatly to pollution and global warming. Because of this threat, along with the unpredictable politics of oil-producing nations, auto engineers have been trying to make gas-powered autos more fuel-efficient. Meanwhile they are trying to produce practical alternatives to gas-powered cars.

ALTERNATIVE FUELS

Rather than gasoline, some automobiles today have other power sources. The U.S. government describes "advanced vehicles and fuels" online at FuelEconomy.gov. They include the following.

- Flexible fuel vehicles (FFVs). FFVs can use a blend of gasoline containing up to 85 percent ethanol (alcohol). Ethanol is less polluting than gasoline but results in fewer miles/kilometers per gallon.
- Diesels. Cars using diesel fuel have been available for many years. The most common type of diesel is derived from petroleum, a fossil fuel, but scientists have developed less-polluting biodiesel blends using biologically grown resources. Diesel fuel costs less than standard gasoline and gets better mileage/kilometrage.

- Hybrids. Hybrid-electric vehicles (HEVs) use gas engines and electric motors together. Power sources can combine for added power when climbing or passing. The hybrid system can improve efficiency with what is called "regenerative braking." The motor helps slow down the wheels; at the same time, energy from the turning of the wheels is converted to electricity to help charge the battery.
- Plug-in hybrids (PHEVs). High-capacity batteries in these vehicles are charged with power cords plugged into electrical outlets and charging stations. Under normal

Cars go through an assembly line at a hybrid motor vehicle plant in Michigan. Hybrid cars combine gasoline engines with electric battery power for improved efficiency.

driving conditions, electrical power notably reduces gas consumption. In some PHEVs, the electric motor and gas engine both propel the car most of the time; at slow speeds, electricity alone can power the car. In others, the electric motor actually propels the wheels while the gas engine generates electricity for the motor; for short trips, no gasoline may be needed.

- All-electric vehicles (EVs). These cars run entirely on electric motors with rechargeable battery units. There are no poisonous emissions (although the power sources from which they are recharged may discharge pollutants). Other benefits are that they require less maintenance than gas engines and run notably quieter. Disadvantages are that they must be recharged every 100 to 200 miles (160 to 320 km)—roughly twice as often as gas-powered cars need refueling—and may take as long as eight hours to recharge; even a partial "quick charge" may take half an hour. Also, battery packs are bulky, heavy, and expensive to replace.

The future of alternative vehicle power systems is a question mark. Scientists continually strive to make advanced vehicles less costly and more efficient.

KEEP TRACK OF YOUR FUEL ECONOMY

Fuel consumption estimates are useful but imperfect indicators. Only after you have driven the car awhile and recorded mileages (kilometrages) in various driving situations can you really know how fuel-efficient your car is. Two cars with identical features, rolled out of the same factory the same day, may yield significantly different driving economies for their owners. Much will depend on the driver and the driving scenario.

The most accurate fuel economy estimates combine "city" and "highway" driving. Basically, city driving involves lots of traffic lights—constant starts and stops. The process of accelerating a vehicle burns extra fuel. Highway driving means you can drive miles and miles before encountering a traffic light or stop sign, resulting in better mileage/kilometrage.

Checking your fuel economy is a simple procedure:

1. Fill the tank completely with gas and jot down the odometer reading.
2. At your next fuel stop, note the odometer reading and fill the tank completely again. Note precisely how much gas it took to refill.
3. Subtract the previous odometer reading from the new one.
4. Divide the number of miles (kilometers) driven between refills by the exact number (including fractions) of gallons/liters it took to fill the tank. This amount reveals how many miles (meters) to the gallon (liter) your car has gotten.

You should check your fuel consumption periodically. Do not be surprised if the numbers vary significantly. Prolonged driving through open country, for example, will reflect better results than daily driving in bumper-to-bumper traffic. However, a notable reduction in mileage/kilometrage suggests the engine, tires, or another system may require servicing.

U.S. DEPARTMENT OF **ENERGY** | Energy Efficiency & Renewable Energy

Office of Transportation & Air Quality | **U.S. ENVIRONMENTAL PROTECTION AGENCY**

www.fueleconomy.gov
the official U.S. government source for fuel economy information

Mobile | Español | Site Map | Links | FAQ | Videos | Contacts

Find a Car   Save Money & Fuel   Benefits   Advanced Vehicles & Fuels   About EPA Ratings   More...

My Trip Calculator

 | **Share**

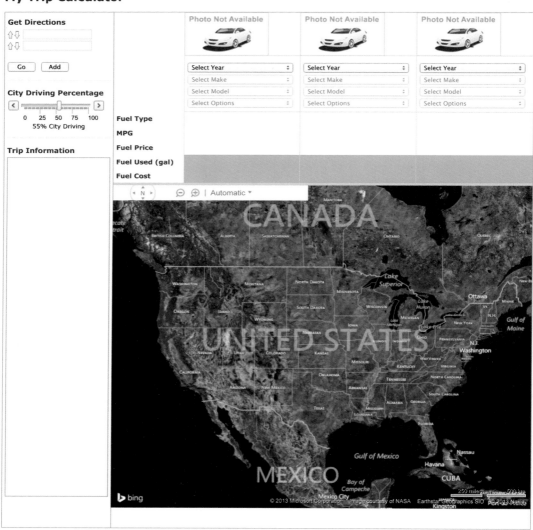

Get Directions

[Go] [Add]

City Driving Percentage

0   25   50   75   100
55% City Driving

Trip Information

Photo Not Available | Photo Not Available | Photo Not Available

Select Year | Select Year | Select Year
Select Make | Select Make | Select Make
Select Model | Select Model | Select Model
Select Options | Select Options | Select Options

Fuel Type
MPG
Fuel Price
Fuel Used (gal)
Fuel Cost

Online apps are available to help motorists monitor their cars' fuel efficiency. "My Trip Calculator," at http://www.fueleconomy.gov, is a service of the U.S. Environmental Protection Agency.

WHAT TO DO WITH AN AGING CAR?

As your car ages, repair costs will mount. Fuel efficiency will diminish. It probably will begin to burn more oil—emitting more pollution. When is it time to trade for a new car or a younger used car?

Like most things in life, it depends. Just because a car has high mileage/kilometrage, the finish is dulled, the upholstery is wearing, and it sometimes sputters on startup does not mean you need to replace it yet.

Cars lose *Kelley Blue Book* value at different rates. Certain models may lose half their original value in a year or two. Others bring nice trade-in prices for their owners after five or even ten years. Generally, they lose most of their initial value in the first four or five years. After that, the rate of loss slows. If you can drive the car ten years or longer without major repairs, you're getting excellent long-term value for your investment.

TIPS TO IMPROVE DRIVING ECONOMY AND CAR HEALTH

The way you drive and the way you treat your car can affect your pocketbook. Keeping the car in top running condition reduces excess pollution. No matter what type of car you buy, it is your responsibility to drive it sensibly and keep it running well. Reckless driving and poor maintenance can lead to higher operating costs and major breakdowns.

Auto experts offer the following advice:

- To conserve fuel, maintain a steady speed whenever possible. Pretend an egg lies behind the accelerator pedal, and avoid crushing the shell. Accelerate gently.
- Have your tires rotated and balanced every 5,000 to 10,000 miles (8,000 to 16,000 km). This step ensures that the treads wear evenly and prolongs the life of the tires.

Tire care includes having tires rotated regularly and the air pressure checked. Proper maintenance can result in better mileage and ensure that the tires last longer.

Tires that never are rotated will wear thin prematurely on the inner or outer edge.

- Check the oil level, using the dipstick under the hood, once a month. Automobiles commonly burn more oil as they age. Failure to maintain the oil level and change the oil regularly can cause serious engine problems.
- When dashboard warning lights come on and stay on, have them checked. Often, a "check engine" warning is caused merely by a glitch in the car's electrical system. It could mean something more ominous, though.

CHAPTER 6

BEYOND THE PURCHASE

The sticker price is just the beginning of what you will pay for the privilege of owning a car. Car costs never end.

INSURANCE, TAXES, AND FEES

The cost of an auto insurance policy is based on various factors. They include the insured person's age, driving record, and health issues that might affect driving. They also include the driver's location, general driving conditions, estimated daily mileage/kilometrage, availability of a protective carport, and so forth. The more comprehensive the coverage, the more expensive the policy will be.

Insurance costs substantially more for young drivers because that age group is involved in a relatively high percentage of accidents. Driver education certification can reduce insurance costs. The AAA provides state-by-state lists of driving schools.

Driving schools simulate a variety of driving scenarios and highway conditions. Successful completion of a driver training course can lower a driver's car insurance cost.

The two main categories of car insurance are collision (in case your car is damaged by another vehicle or an act of nature) and liability (in case your car is the cause of damage or injury in an accident). Even with an insurance policy, the owner usually has to pay a portion of the repair, known as the deductible.

Suppose your insurance policy's deductible amount is $1,000. A tree limb falls on your car hood. If the repair estimate is $950, your insurance company won't pay any of it. If the repair costs $1,100, you must pay $1,000; the insurer will pay the remaining $100.

You can buy a policy with a lower deductible. This type will be to your advantage when only slight damage occurs, but the policy will cost more. When shopping for car insurance, you want to find the policy that 1) provides comprehensive coverage, 2) carries a low deductible, and 3) is modestly priced.

The owner must pay an annual or biannual car registration and license plate fee to the state division of motor vehicles. County taxes must be currently paid to renew auto registration. Every few years, drivers must renew their licenses. This renewal usually requires passing a vision test and costs a small fee. Any time you are stopped by a traffic officer, you probably will be asked to show your driver's license and vehicle registration. Failure to have either of them available can result in arrest and a fine. Other fees in certain states include that for an annual car inspection by a state-approved mechanic.

FUEL

Fuel is the major after-purchase expense. Future costs are difficult to estimate because of uncertain fluctuations in petroleum and gas prices. It is wise to budget more for fuel than may seem necessary based on this week's pump prices.

The U.S. Department of Energy posts an online fuel cost calculator (http://www.fueleconomy.gov/feg/savemoney.shtml). You can enter the average fuel price in your area, your car's average mileage, the number of miles you expect to drive in a year, and the number of years you plan to own the car. Click "Calculate," and the app instantly estimates your annual fuel costs and the total fuel costs for the life of the vehicle.

As an example, assume long-term fuel prices will average $3.10 per gallon. At that pump price, a car that averages 27 MPG, if driven 15,000 miles annually, will consume $1,722 worth of fuel in a year. If driven for five years and the numbers (fuel prices, MPG average, and number of miles driven annually) hold constant, fuel will cost the owner $8,611 in the span of five years. Depending on a car's fuel economy and how long it is driven, fuel conceivably could cost the owner more than the car's purchase price.

The calculator is an imperfect predictor because each of the variables may shift markedly over the course of a year or longer. It provides a good idea, though, of how much you should budget for fuel. It is also an excellent tool for comparing how much more or less fuel will cost for cars with differing economy ratings.

KEEP A CAR CARE CALENDAR

TO MAKE SURE YOU STAY UP TO DATE WITH RECURRING CAR-RELATED RESPONSIBILITIES, RECORD REGULAR TO-DO ITEMS ON YOUR CALENDAR OR IN A CAR SCHEDULING APP. REMINDERS MAY INCLUDE LOAN AND INSURANCE PAYMENT DATES, OIL CHANGES EVERY THREE MONTHS, TIRE ROTATIONS EVERY SIX MONTHS, ETC.

THE AAA OFFERS A FREE E-MAIL REMINDER PROGRAM AT AAA.COM. THE AAA AUTOMANAGER APPLICATION SENDS E-MAIL NOTICES OF SCHEDULED TASKS SUCH AS THOSE ABOVE. IT ALSO MONITORS VEHICLE RECALL NOTICES.

MAINTENANCE

The oil in the car should be changed approximately every 3,000 to 5,000 miles (4,800 to 8,000 km). Many oil change stations also provide basic engine checks and tune-ups, such as checking valves and sparkplugs and cleaning or replacing air and fuel filters. This regular maintenance is usually inexpensive: $25 to $50, depending on the class and model of car, plus the cost of replacement items.

Be wary when taking your car in for routine service and being told the vehicle needs unforeseen repairs. The engine may need a new air filter, brake fluid change, or transmission flush ahead of the manufacturer's recommended maintenance schedule—or not. Find a shop you can trust not to perform unnecessary work.

For new cars, major maintenance at the dealership is typically called for at 30,000 and/or 60,000 miles (48,000 and/or 96,000 km), with less extensive servicing at other intervals. These service visits include thorough testing of the engine, brakes, emission, and other systems. At certain points, they entail replacing parts such as the timing belt. With some new cars, maintenance is provided free for a certain period of time or number of miles.

You will probably need to buy new tires approximately every 30,000 to 60,000 miles (48,000 to 96,000 km). Most tire dealers include mounting and balancing each tire in the total price. Tires should be rotated at least twice a year—more often on cars that accumulate above-average mileage. Many tire sellers

A mechanic performs a routine oil change—a major component of regular auto maintenance. Proper maintenance can prevent major malfunctions and prolong the life of a vehicle.

offer to perform maintenance tasks free for the life of the tire. New tires typically come with some form of guarantee.

Brake systems generally need attention after several years—sooner for high-mileage/kilometrage vehicles. Some brake jobs involve only the replacement of pads or liners on front or rear brakes. Others require complete overhauls.

Two separate costs are involved in maintenance and repairs: parts and labor. "Parts" can vary from four quarts of oil and a new filter during a routine oil change to a replacement radiator, engine block, or catalytic converter.

MINOR AND MAJOR REPAIRS

Some auto repairs are easy and inexpensive; you may be able to perform them yourself. Others are involved and costly; only experienced mechanics can handle them.

Failure of the engine to start might result from any number of issues. The repair may be as quick and simple as scraping and cleaning corroded battery cables. If the battery is older than five years, it may have to be replaced. Owners can buy and install a new battery themselves—but before they do, they must test the old battery to confirm it is really the problem. Owners can buy and learn to use testing devices, too. Most drivers draw the self-help line at this juncture, however, preferring to turn the problem over to a professional mechanic or at least to a car-savvy friend.

Using a diagnostic testing device, a mechanic checks for problems under the hood. Computerized testing can pinpoint the causes of mysterious malfunctions.

Many owners take their cars to a garage or to the dealership's service department for all routine maintenance and for even the slightest repairs. If you are willing to learn to perform certain maintenance and minor repair tasks, you can save significant money over the years.

Major repairs can be done only by automotive professionals. Examples are brake jobs and extensive work on the engine, cooling system, emission system, and so forth.

Take note that when costly repairs are needed, the quality of replacement parts can have lasting effects. A replacement part made by the car manufacturer may cost $1,500; a local mechanic can get you an aftermarket substitute (made by an independent company) for half the price. But eventually, the substitute part might cause problems with related parts.

CAR OWNERSHIP: A WORTHY GOAL

Not every high school or college student needs a car. Not every family can afford to supply a student with his or her own set of wheels. Car ownership is a dream of many teenagers, but it may be unattainable until they begin full-time careers. Even if it is doable now, it's wise to postpone a car purchase until it's truly necessary. If walking, bicycling, ride sharing, or mass-transit systems suffice, use them.

When they do get behind the wheel of their own car, young owners soon realize car ownership is an expensive and at times frustrating experience. But the car is also liberating, enjoyable, and extremely useful. Owning a car is a goal worth pursuing.

amortization The paying off of debt in regular installments over a period of time.

biannual Occurring twice each year.

cabriolet A two-door convertible.

car title Certificate of ownership.

comprehensive coverage Complete or extensive insurance coverage.

credit rating The determination of a person's level of lending risk based on income, debt, record of timely payments, etc.

deductible The first portion of damage or injury costs that the insured person must pay before the insurance company assumes coverage.

defensive driving Deliberately driving in such a way as to reduce the risk of accidents.

electronic stability control Technology that detects and automatically helps correct skidding.

ethanol Pure alcohol; it can be used as auto fuel.

fossil fuel A category of fuel such as petroleum that was created over many millennia from plant and animal fossils.

hatchback A small car with a rear door that opens vertically.

odometer An instrument on the dashboard that records the number of miles/kilometers a vehicle is driven.

petroleum Crude oil brought up from beneath Earth's surface.

rebate A portion of the car purchase amount paid back to the buyer.

sedan A two- or four-door car of average size and with both front and back seats.

warranty A guarantee by the seller or manufacturer to freely replace or repair faulty car parts for a period of time.

American Automobile Association (AAA)
1000 AAA Drive
Heathrow, FL 32746
(407) 444-8000
Website: http://www.aaa.com
The federation of auto clubs provides a wealth of information and tips for drivers and automobile shoppers.

Americans Well-informed on Automobile Retailing Economics (AWARE)
919 18th Street NW, Suite 300
Washington, DC 20006
(202) 888-2082
Website: http://www.autofinancing101.org
Among other resources, AWARE provides an online auto-finance calculator and a variety of interactive vehicle finance educational tools.

Auto123.com
420 Armand-Frappier, Suite 200
Laval, QC H7V 4B4
Canada
(866) 669-1305
Website: http://www.auto123.com
This Canadian automotive portal provides helpful information for car drivers and enthusiasts.

Consumer Reports
Consumers Union
101 Truman Avenue
Yonkers, NY 10703-1057
(914) 378-2000
Website: http://www.consumerrports.org
Consumer Reports is a nonprofit organization dedicated to improving the marketplace for consumers. It tests thousands of products, including autos.

Council of Better Business Bureaus (BBB)
3033 Wilson Boulevard, Suite 600
Arlington, VA 22201
(703) 276-0100
Website: http://www.bbb.org
The BBB provides alerts, tips, and a video library to educate consumers. Its Web site includes the BBB auto line service (www.bbb.org/us/auto-line-lemon-law) where car owners can file lemon law complaints.

Federal Trade Commission (FTC)
600 Pennsylvania Avenue NW
Washington, DC 20580
(202) 326-2222
Website: http://www.ftc.gov
The FTC's auto-related information and guidance include material on carmakers and on auto advertising, purchasing, and contracts.

National Automobile Dealers Association (NADA)
8400 Westpark Drive
McLean, VA 22102
(703) 821-7000
Website: http://www.nada.org
This organization provides information on safety, financing, and other auto-related topics.

National Highway Traffic Safety Administration (NHTSA)
1200 New Jersey Avenue SE, West Building
Washington, DC 20590
(888) 327-4326
Website: http://www.nhtsa.gov
Since 1970, the NHTSA has worked with drivers "to help prevent crashes and their attendant costs, both human and financial."

WEBSITES

Due to the changing nature of Internet links, Rosen Publishing has developed an online list of websites related to the subject of this book. This site is updated regularly. Please use this link to access the list:

http://www.rosenlinks.com/FSLS/Car

FOR FURTHER READING

Berg, David W., and Meg Green. *Savings and Investments* (Dollars and Sense: A Guide to Financial Literacy). New York, NY: Rosen Publishing, 2012.

Butler, Tamsen. *The Complete Guide to Personal Finance: For Teenagers and College Students*. Ocala, FL: Atlantic Publishing, 2010.

Chatzky, Jean. *Not Your Parents' Money Book: Making, Saving, and Spending Your Own Money*. New York, NY: Simon & Schuster Books for Young Readers, 2010.

Denega, Danielle. *Smart Money* (How to Manage Your Cash). New York, NY: Franklin Watts, 2008.

Fix, Lauren. *Lauren Fix's Guide to Loving Your Car: Everything You Need to Know to Take Charge of Your Car and Get On with Your Life*. New York, NY: St. Martin's Press, 2008.

Harmon, Daniel E. *First Car Smarts* (Get $mart with Your Money). New York, NY: Rosen Publishing, 2010.

Monteverde, Matt. *Frequently Asked Questions About Budgeting and Money Management* (FAQ: Teen Life). New York, NY: Rosen Publishing, 2009.

Munroe, Brian. *Car Buying Revealed: How to Buy a Car and Not Get Taken for a Ride*. Garden City, NJ: Morgan James Publishing, 2008.

Orr, Tamra. *A Kid's Guide to the Economy* (Money Matters: A Kid's Guide to Money). Hockessin, DE: Mitchell Lane Publishers, 2010.

Peterson, Judy Monroe. *First Budget Smarts* (Get $mart with Your Money). New York, NY: Rosen Publishing, 2010 .

Stalder, Erika. *In the Driver's Seat: A Girl's Guide to Her First Car*. San Francisco, CA: Zest Books, 2009.

BIBLIOGRAPHY

"AAA StartSmart Parent-Teen Driving Agreement." American Automobile Association. Retrieved November 2013 (http://teendriving.aaa.com/files/file/Parent.Teen.Driving.Agreement.pdf).

Alexander, Brian. "Car Maintenance: What to Expect at Each Service Level." DriverSide.com. Retrieved November 2013 (http://www.driverside.com/auto-library/car_maintenance _what_to_expect_at_each_service_interval-26).

AutoTrader.com. "AutoTrader.com Study Reveals Deep Insights into How Millennials Relate to Cars." August 23, 2013. Retrieved November 2013 (http://press.autotrader.com/ 2013-08-23-AutoTrader-com-Study-Reveals-Deep -Insights-into-how-Millennials-Relate-to-Cars).

"The Big Expense Hiding in the Driveway." Energy Trap.org. Retrieved November 2013 (http://stories.energytrap.org/ annualcost).

Eisenstein, Paul A. "New Cars Increasingly Out of Reach for Many Americans." NBC News/CNBC, February 27, 2013. Retrieved October 2013 (http://finance.yahoo.com/news/ cars-increasingly-reach-many-americans-145957880.html).

"Extended Warranties and Service Contracts." Federal Trade Commission/Consumer Information. Retrieved November 2013 (http://www.consumer.ftc.gov/articles/0240- extended-warranties-and-service-contracts).

"Keys2Drive: The AAA Guide to Teen Driver Safety." Retrieved November 2013 (http://teendriving.aaa.com.)

Lawrence, Judy. *The Budget Kit*. 6th ed. New York, NY: Kaplan Publishing, 2011.

Mays, Kelsey. "Making Sense of New-Car Warranties." Cars.
com, June 4, 2013. Retrieved November 2013 (http://
www.cars.com/go/advice/Story.jsp?section=buy&subject
=warranty).

"Save Money with a Manual Transmission." *Consumer Reports*, February 2013. Retrieved November 2013 (http://
www.consumerreports.org/cro/2012/01/save-gas-and
-money-with-a-manual-transmission/index.htm).

"So Your Teen Wants a Car? A Parent's Guide to Choosing a Vehicle." AAA brochure. Retrieved November
2013 (http://teendriving.aaa.com/files/file/
SoYourTeenWantsaCar.08.pdf).

"Turning Teens' Quest for First Set of Wheels Into an
Educational Opportunity." Americans Well-Informed
on Automobile Retail Economics press release, July
30, 2013. Retrieved November 22, 2013 (http://www.
autofinancing101.org/media_center/files/Teens%20
Seeking%20First%20Set%20of%20Wheels%20July%20
2013%20FINAL.pdf).

Tuttle, Brad. "Bargain Car-Buying Season: Best Affordable
New Vehicles, and Strategies for Getting Them Cheap."
Time, November 18, 2010. Retrieved November 2013
(http://business.time.com/2010/11/18/bargain-car-buy-
ing-season-best-affordable-new-vehicles-and-strategies-
for-getting-them-cheap).

"Your Driving Costs: How Much Are You Really Paying to
Drive?" Heathrow, FL: American Automobile Association, 2010.

INDEX

A

accidents, 14, 18, 63
all-electric vehicles, 56
alternative fuels, 54–56
American Automobile Association
  (AAA), 7, 9, 14, 17, 42, 43,
  44, 45, 48, 62, 65
amortization programs, 35
auto industry
  overview of current, 20–22

B

budgeting, 14, 36–38, 48

C

carbon dioxide, 54
car care calendars, 65
carpooling, 12
cars
  affordability, 42, 44–45
  calculating the value of, 25–27
  deciding whether buying is best,
    12–14
  driving safely, 14, 16–17, 43, 59
  extending the life of, 59–61
  familiarity, 42, 45
  features to choose, 22, 24–25
  myths about cars and driving,
    18–19
  reasons for high quality of cur-
    rent, 21–22
  reliability, 42, 45

safest vehicles, 42, 43
teens and, 15, 23
types of, 42–43

D

diesels, 54
Dodge Dart Registry, 35
down payments, 13, 30, 34, 36,
  37, 48
driving under the influence, 16

E

electronic stability control, 43
environment
  automobiles and impact on the,
    17, 52–53

F

financing, 32–35
flexible fuel vehicles, 54
Ford, Henry, 10
fuel
  costs of, 8, 30, 38, 45, 64–65
  keeping a record of consump-
    tion, 56–57

H

hybrids, 55

I

insurance, 8, 40, 45, 62–64, 65
interest, 34–35
invoice price, 31

ABOUT THE AUTHOR

Daniel E. Harmon is the author of more than eighty books and thousands of articles on varied topics. He has also written the books *First Car Smarts* and *First Job Smarts* for young adults. A resident of Spartanburg, South Carolina, Harmon always has driven subcompact economy cars.

PHOTO CREDITS

Cover, p. 3 Willie B. Thomas/E+/ Getty Images; pp. 6–7 Troels Graugaard/E+/Getty Images; p. 11 cleanfotos/Shutterstock.com; p. 13 Ryan McVay/Photodisc/Thinkstock; p. 16 Tetra Images/Getty Images; p. 21 Frederic J. Brown/AFP/Getty Images; p. 24 kaczor58/Shutterstock.com; p. 27 PRNewsFoto/Kelly Blue Book/AP Images; p. 31 JGI/Blend Images/Getty Images; p. 33 © AP Images; p. 37 Andrey Popov/Shutterstock.com; p. 42 Jonathan Ernst/Reuters/Landov; p. 44 Krystof Kriz/CTK/AP Images; p. 46 Bloomberg/Getty Images; p. 50 Miodrag Gajic/E+/Getty Images; p. 53 Melinda Fawver/Shutterstock.com; p. 55 Bill Pugliano/Getty Images; p. 60 Adam Gault/OJO Images/Getty Images; p. 63 Chuck Crow/The Plain Dealer/Landov; p. 67 Jupiterimages/Stockbyte/Thinkstock; p. 69 Peter Dazeley/Iconica/Getty Images; interior page design elements © iStockphoto.com/yystom (arrows), © iStockphoto.com/JLGutierrez (financial terms), © iStockphoto.com/ahlobystov (numbers).

Designer: Nelson Sá; Editor: Kathy Kuhtz Campbell;
Photo Researcher: Marty Levick